The Little Book of Wholeness and Prayer

The Little Book of Wholeness and Prayer

AN EIGHT-WEEK MEDITATION GUIDE

KIMBERLY BEYER-NELSON

SKINNER HOUSE BOOKS
BOSTON

 Published by Skinner House Books. Skinner House Books is an imprint of the Unitarian Universalist Association, a liberal religious organization with more than 1,000 congregations in the U.S. and Canada. 25 Beacon Street, Boston, MA 02108-2800.

Printed in Canada

Cover design by Kathryn Sky-Peck
Text design by Sandra Rigney

ISBN 1-55896-436-3

Library of Congress Cataloging-in-Publication Data

Beyer-Nelson, Kimberly.
The little book of wholeness and prayer: an eight-week meditation guide / Kimberly Beyer-Nelson.
p. cm.
Includes bibliographical references (p.).
ISBN 1-55896-436-3 (alk. paper)
I. Title.

BV4813.B49 2002
291.4'3—dc21 2002021243

5 4 3 2 1

05 04 03 02

Contents

Introduction vii

Week One 1

Week Two 15

Week Three 33

Week Four 49

Week Five 65

Week Six 79

Week Seven 93

Week Eight 107

Resources 121

Introduction

This guide is an invitation to explore how spirituality is integral to the implementation of holistic health practices. Choice is the root of responsibility, and good choices require us to be aware and mindful. When you act out of a quiet center of clarity, you can respond more authentically to the needs of your mind, body, and spirit, as well as to the needs of others. In a sense, the only real way to wholeness is through such deep awareness. Brian Luke Seaward, in his book *Stand Like Mountain, Flow Like Water*, writes, "The word health comes to us from the Anglican word 'hal,' meaning to be whole or holy. One cannot speak of health without understanding human spirituality. For spiritual fitness is inextricably linked to our mental, emotional and physical health."

And that wholeness doesn't mean being free of illness. Often, illness is simply beyond anyone's control. Rather, wholeness happens when mind, body, and spirit are brought into full awareness and, more importantly, into the embrace of your full acceptance. Illness may very well be part of your personal life journey. It will be for most of us at some point. *Holistic health* means being open to the wisdom of health *and* illness, making choices that reflect the reality of your life, to finding in these experiences the textures and meanings of what it is to be a fully embodied and engaged human being.

Unlike a simple clutch of meditations, this guide invites you to become an active partner in the experience of your whole-body relationship with God. Doing so should entail a kind of freedom for you. No one will see the pictures that you may draw, or read about the little personal foibles you may have uncovered, unless you choose to share your insights. As you work through this book, do what you feel called to do, integrate the elements that make sense to you, and leave the rest. It will become, when all is said and done, a journey into the process of discernment. You may find that working through this book will move you into sacred time, a time for you to explore, create, and integrate the elements of a holistic lifestyle into the daily rhythms of your life. This work will create a forum for you to shift from an intellectual understanding of health and spirit into the deeper learning of participation.

Throughout this book, you will find pages specifically set aside for your thoughts, your sketches, or even those few bars of music that come calling. I encourage you to exercise your intellect and your creativity as you work through this text. Reviewing your entries weeks, months, or even years from now will give you fresh insights into your own personal and spiritual evolution.

I gave birth to this book some years ago, during a time of sweeping changes in my life. I had divorced, remarried, been involved in a major car accident, moved seven times in the span of two years, broke my left foot not once but twice, started and completed graduate work—the changes and challenges went on and on. I'm not afraid to say it was the most stressful and heartrending time of my life.

Yet over time, a slow, but inexorable, healing began. Sitting in my study one brilliant autumn morning, staring out across Asylum Lake, I realized that part of the process of finding peace within and without had to do with relearning to spiritualize every aspect of my life. While I had implemented gentle lifestyle changes and explored painful pieces of my personality, the key to finding a lasting peace had come with the creation of a prayer vessel that could hold change. It was a place where an internal alchemy could work its magic. Watching the autumn leaves drift on fingers of wind beyond my sliding door, I resolved to capture this process in a way that could challenge and encourage others. So each day for eight weeks, I turned my fingers to a blank white computer screen, and this book is the result.

My notion of the divine has changed through the years. That which I call *God* others might call *Tao*, or *Dharmakaya*, or simply *the universe*. Whatever the name, it is a presence beyond gender, form, and complete understanding. I find, though, that I must include a sense of the personal, the relational, and the near in my meaning of God. For me, God has a decidedly feminine nature. She is the creator and the destroyer, sharing in aspects of the universal divine that I recognize and honor in my own fragile life. And even as I acknowledge that God had a hand in shaping me, I also have a creative interest in how I, in turn, mold my ever-evolving image of the divine.

This guide is not about getting in touch with a divine that is somehow outside us or transcendent. Rather, it is a work that attempts to clarify how God is immanent in all aspects of our lives, and to help you explore what that means to you as an individual.

Most of us understand that the words *holistic health* refer to all the pieces of our lives working together as a system. This living system includes the foods we choose to eat, the music we make, the thoughts we say to ourselves throughout the day, and our relationships with others. All of these interact to affect our sense of wholeness, health, and fulfillment of the mind, body, and spirit. We know we should eat better; we understand that humor and play are integral parts of living; we've wrestled with difficult emotions and have some sense of how our thoughts and actions affect our lives. Yet how do we begin to move beyond merely understanding these concepts into actually living in a way that honors what our minds already know? Working through this guide, I hope you will find the answers to these questions.

A few years back when changes battered my mind and heart, I learned to gather all the ambiguity and fears of those times and sit with them in meditation. I didn't try to fix anything. I didn't try to make sense out of anything. My prayer life was simple then. I shut my eyes and let myself just be held by God. Following the counsel of Thomas Keating, a Trappist monk, I chose a single word that directed my attention back to the divine again, again, and again.

I found that all prayer is not energetically the same. Chanting the names of God, sending healing prayers out to a sick friend, structuring wild energy with the discipline of Hatha Yoga, and entering into contemplation are all concrete movements of the dance between oneself and God. Each form has a specific feel and a specific intent, even though all may be considered kinds of prayer.

In this book, you will encounter three categories of prayer: active contemplation, verbal prayer, and centering prayer. These prayer categories are simply a way to create a common language between us for the purposes of this work, because prayer has many different names, including *contemplation*, *meditation*, and *invocation*. There is a Hindu teaching story that goes something like this:

> A young devotee, after spending a hot and dusty day touring the myriad temples of his city, asks his spiritual teacher, "How many gods people this universe of ours?"
>
> "A billion billion gods," the old woman answers immediately.
>
> "Truly?" the devotee asks with wide eyes.
>
> "Well, perhaps only thirty-three."
>
> "Thirty-three," the devotee repeats, his brow furrowing. "But what is the truth?"
>
> The old woman smiles then, in a flash of white teeth. "Truthfully? Only one."

For each of us, there will be a unique understanding of God, as well as a unique style for interacting with the divine. And yes, the practice of prayer is complex, and at the same time it is simple. In the end, day by day, prayer by prayer, you can choose the form that best suits you. The many are the one when brought to their common denominator.

The following is a brief introduction to the categories of prayer you will encounter in this book. Use them as they suit you.

Active Contemplation

Active contemplation is analytical thought, interaction with the words of sacred or secular literature, or thoughts spurred on by experience in the world. You might be surprised to consider such musings as a kind of prayer. Yet if our thoughts—our ideas and mental connections—are bent on seeing more clearly into our reality, such activities do indeed become a kind of meditation. We can contemplate our day-to-day activities, readings, and comings and goings and find in them a better understanding of the sacred. But in our quest for a better understanding of wholeness, this may be just the beginning. Thomas Merton cautions, "The activity proper to man is not purely mental because man is not just a disembodied mind. Our destiny is to live out what we think, because unless we live what we know, we do not even know it."

Verbal Prayer

When we shift to a conversation with the sacred, however we understand it, we take one more step toward knowing ourselves more fully. Speech is the active way we engage with the world, create relationships, share stories, reveal truths. Verbal prayer, written or spoken, can take many forms. Many you will recognize from their somewhat established places in worship services; others are more often associated with private prayer.

Prayers of invocation are calls for the divine to be present in our awareness. They are words that signify that we are opening ourselves to the presence of whatever we consider holy. An invocation might be something like "Welcome, creative spirit! I come to this time seeking to be present and clear in my life."

Prayers of petition are requests directed at the sacred on behalf of ourselves. Perhaps we are frightened by a thunderstorm, and we ask for strength. These prayers express our relationship with the world and with our spiritual selves.

Prayers of intercession are offered on behalf of others. Your aunt is sick, and you pray that the divine will support her through the illness. While a prayer of intercession may help the other person (and more and more actual research on the subject supports the idea that it does), it also fulfills our own need to help and care for others. As such, it is a prayer form that turns us outward as active and transformational forces in the world.

Prayers of lament are offered out of our brokenness or anger. A full relationship with our world asks us to be honest with the full spectrum of our human experiences. When you have been through the death of a loved one, or lost an important job, or become estranged from your child, the natural and healing prayer of lament allows you to give voice to this pain: "I feel broken and lonely and angry today. I shall stay open to what these emotions might be trying to tell me, without running away from them."

Prayers of celebration, thanksgiving, and awe are essentially celebrations of life. You might say something like, "What a beautiful day I have awakened to! I hear you, bird! And sun! Such light! How can I not feel, in some way, blessed?" These words celebrate the miracle of life and mark the points where we have awakened from daily routine into a precious moment of gratitude.

Often our verbal prayers include some or all features of these prayer types. We may seek after the wisdom to confront a personal problem that is hounding us, pray for loved ones who are ill, and give thanks for the presence of love in our lives. As we do, we are experiencing the textures of our own emotional and spiritual selves. By inviting our understanding of the divine into this framework, we come to better know and understand our selves in the widest sense of the word.

Centering Prayer

The practice of centering, or contemplative, prayer comes to us from about the fourteenth century, primarily through an anonymous work called *The Cloud of Unknowing* and the works of Saint Teresa of Avila. But the roots of this contemplative prayer go even farther back, to Evagrius of Pontus (345 C.E.), one of the Desert Fathers. Father Thomas Keating has been instrumental in reviving these ancient traditions in what he calls *centering prayer*. In an article in *Common Boundary* entitled "Resting in God," Anne A. Simpkinson notes that Keating "deeply grasped the fact that Christianity was a contemplative religion. He realized that the spiritual sense of the Scripture was much more important than the literal and that union with the Divine was not only possible but available to all." But centering prayer does not require a Christian orientation. We can bring our own understanding of the divine to this prayer form.

Centering prayer is a kind of letting go, through which we can enter into the deep interior of our lives. Whereas active contemplation tends to concern our own thoughts and verbal prayer expresses a relational dialogue, centering prayer is simply quieting the self and listening within. Keating writes, "Every response to God, whatever it is, must begin with the full acceptance of reality as it actually is at the moment." The practice of centering prayer in its stillness and abiding is a way to begin to bring present mindfulness into our relationship with ourselves and the divine.

Getting Started with Centering Prayer

To begin with centering prayer, choose a word that is sacred to you. This word will be your concentration point, and you should not change it once your prayer has begun. The point of this kind of prayer is to move away from thought, and changing your word means that you are again thinking and acting on your thinking. Some people prefer to use words such as *Father*, *Spirit*, or *amen*, but more secular words can be equally useful. Such words might include *one*, *peace*, or *calm*. The word is an intention—a finger pointing you toward the divine. Your word declares your intention to be open and aware, committed to the inward journey.

Find a comfortable position, either on a chair or on the floor. If you are sitting, keep your back straight. If you lie down, be aware you may be more prone to falling asleep.

Close your eyes. Gently breathe your chosen word across your conscious mind. As thoughts arise, let them go by, silently saying your sacred word and returning to the quiet. Your word is a reminder to return to the presence of God when you realize your mind is distracted. You cannot really still your thoughts. They will arise, because that is the nature of your mind. But you can choose not to follow them, not to become emotionally engaged in them. In a sense, you are catching a thought before it becomes a full story. For instance, images of an impending shopping trip surface, you start to plan the list of things to do, and then you catch yourself. You breathe your word and let go, coming back with renewed focus and intent. Gradually, you may find that you can see the rise and fall of your thoughts without developing them into story lines. This point is where the real quiet and healing begin. You may experience a slower heartbeat and fewer breaths per minute. Research tells us that in deep meditation, oxygen consumption slows and levels of immune factors rise. In this state we receive more real rest than we do in sleep. Meditation is a healing activity on many different levels.

At the end of the prayer session, spend a moment in silence, perhaps introducing a silent *amen* or another concluding word. Let your external senses return gradually. By not rushing, you are able to bring this peace and silence back into your daily life.

This kind of prayer is an exercise in attention and awareness. The quality of your prayer can change from day to day, depending upon your mood, the pace and activities of the day, or even whether you have eaten or not. Centering prayer is not about attainment, about getting somewhere or achieving something. Rather, it is about being in the present, in each moment, and about honoring that experience as good and right and even holy. The prayer practice develops our ability to be aware, awake, and focused. By sitting honestly with ourselves and God, allowing silence into our lives, we can enlarge our capacity to accept and love ourselves as we find ourselves each day.

It is not uncommon to experience uncomfortable emotions or memories during this practice. By seeking silence, our thoughts and emotions have a tendency to rise and find their own voices. Sometimes issues from our past that we have not dealt with or hurtful feelings can seem overpowering. These sharp thoughts and feelings are just that, thoughts and feelings. Centering prayer teaches us to be aware and then let go. If the presence of uncomfortable feelings becomes deeply troublesome for you, find someone who can support you in your experience. A minister, a counselor, or a close friend can help you talk out the feelings and thoughts. By choosing to work on this material, you can guide yourself to further wholeness.

Keating suggests two twenty-minute periods of centering prayer daily. In this guide we will start more gradually, with shorter periods that can be extended if you choose. Your practice should reflect your own inner wisdom. As always, do what you feel called to do.

How the Book Is Organized

In this book, each day begins with a text that frames the exercises for the day. These quoted texts, from a variety of sources, are offered to promote insight and begin the process of engaging your experiences directly. You will notice that the book provides specific explorations for six days of the week. I am honoring the idea that the seventh day is a time for community, rest, and play. Does that mean you should take yourself off to church? Not necessarily. But I do hope you will find some way to touch the spirit of your life and others in a way that is wholly you on this seventh day.

"Contemplation" is the "doing" part of the day's activity. Sometimes you will be asked to listen to a piece of music; other times you may draw a cartoon or simply hold a leaf. You will be invited to write about your experiences in your journal, giving form and expression to your inner discoveries.

Next, in the "Verbal Prayer," you will be invited to speak or write verbal prayer. Various forms of verbal prayer will be suggested. Remember, the suggestions are given to help you. If you feel that you need to explore a path that seems to diverge from the day's suggested prayer topics, please trust this intuition! You may also wish to write your prayers in your journal as touchstones for later contemplation.

"Centering Prayer" concludes each activity page. This is a time of quiet and wordless relationship between yourself and Spirit. We will start out with about ten minutes of such prayer and gradually increase that to twenty minutes per day.

At the back of the book you will find the Resources, a list of recommended readings grouped by subject.

The Journal

As you move through this book you will find that each day's exercise invites you to write words or draw pictures that capture the feelings, memories, or longings that the day's contemplation inspires. Know that when you put words or images on the page, you are invoking a kind of awareness and intention. Sometimes we carry with us a heavy load of largely unconscious beliefs about the world or ourselves, pockets of grief that we have shoved away, anger that we have buried deeply, or joy and gratitude that we do not often express. The act of writing or drawing helps us uncover these parts of ourselves and brings them into focus, holds them intentionally in our consciousness, where they can be actively worked with.

You may finish the eight weeks with very few journal entries, or you may find that you have filled all of the blank pages provided in this book. In any case, be aware that consciously writing down your thoughts, scribbling a favorite quote, or sketching out a cartoon brings your full attention to the page and to the idea. In so doing, you will probably experience a little moment when you aren't worrying about the future or the past. What you create in your journal at that moment is a slice of real time—a way you can begin to experience the present moment in a new way.

The Place

You will need a place where you can work undisturbed. It might be your bedroom, a corner of your living room, the dining room table, or your favorite chair. Maybe you have a park bench you can go to at lunchtime, or perhaps you are blessed with a lake where you can sit beside the water and write. Wherever you choose, make this your place to come to alone as you work through this book. You won't want to be distracted by the phone or the demands of others during this time. You should feel both a sense of comfort and a feeling of sacredness in your special place. You may wish to add a candle or some fresh flowers. Some people find that simply bringing themselves and their intention to be present to their spiritual journey creates a sense of the sacred for them. Follow what you feel is best.

Sometimes the exercises in this book will ask you to move your body, choose an item from your kitchen, or listen to a piece of music. After this activity, come back to your place to reflect and write about your experiences. Maybe the activity will have triggered a particular emotion, or maybe you will feel inspired to write a poem, doodle, or write about a powerful memory that is reawakened. Or perhaps nothing at all will strike you during the session. That nothingness is an equally fruitful place to begin self-inquiry. Allow yourself the room to be honest about what you do or do not wish to acknowledge or express on a given day.

Let's begin the journey!

Week One

DAY ONE

Waking up this morning, I smile.
Twenty-four brand new hours are before me.
I vow to live fully in each moment
and to look at all beings with eyes of compassion.

Thich Nhat Hahn, *Present Moment, Wonderful Moment*

Contemplation

For a moment, run your fingers over the texture of your own hand. Be aware of the soft twist of veins folding around bone and the feel of the skin (Is it dry? Moist?). Notice the coolness or warmth you find there. Flex your fingers wide. How does this feel to your body? To your emotions? Close your fingers into a fist. Again, how does this feel? Make an OK sign by bringing your pointer finger and thumb together for a moment; then stick your thumb in the air in the "thumbs up" gesture. (Don't worry, no one will laugh!) Write in your journal about all the things your hand does each day.

Verbal Prayer

Share what you learned when you focused on your hand. Did you see something new in yourself? Does the hand, with its range of motion and ability to express feelings, call you to service? To praise? To create? How does personal will express itself in your hand? How does the hand partner with surrender or acceptance? How does your hand engage in relationship with others throughout the day?

Today spend ten minutes on centering prayer. You may find it helpful to refer back to the introduction of this book and carefully review the instructions for centering prayer found there.

DAY TWO

> Only in a prosperous society could we ever forget that food is one of life's primary blessings. I am one who sometimes forgets and takes food for granted, but I'm grateful when I remember that food is precious.
>
> John Robbins, *May All Be Fed*

Contemplation

Think back to the meal or snack you have most recently finished. Can you easily recall the textures and tastes you experienced? Think for a moment about how you prepared the food. What thoughts or feelings were within you as you cooked, sliced, opened, and poured? Perhaps you ate your most recent meal in a restaurant. How did you decide what to select from the menu? What sensations did you experience when your food was presented to you at your table? So often, we miss the miracle of food, the joy of the preparation, the colors, the smells. As John Robbins says, we often forget and take food for granted. Next time you prepare food for yourself or others, or sit down to a restaurant meal, take just a moment to really experience your food with all of your senses. You might be surprised at the richness you find there.

Verbal Prayer

Celebrate the gift of food by writing a short poem or drawing a picture. What things could you do to help you awaken to the miracle of preparing food and sharing meals? Share the stumbling blocks you experience when you try to stay focused on food preparation or the experience of a meal. Perhaps you recently consumed a meal that was less than nutritious or are often in a lunchtime rush of cellular phone calls and loud music. How do such experiences affect you mentally, emotionally, or spiritually?

Today spend ten minutes on centering prayer.

DAY THREE

> If we ask what literature is about, we have to answer that it is about the mystery of the human heart and its passage through time.
>
> Hugh Dinwiddy, *The Springs of Morality*

Contemplation

Today, summon to mind a few words from literature or poetry. Your recall doesn't have to be letter perfect; simply relate some grains of wisdom that you remember. You can write them here in the space provided. If nothing comes at once, don't fret. Simply stay open throughout the day to the impact of words you come across in the midst of your life. Or go to a favorite book and slowly read a passage at random, writing down a phrase that strikes an emotional or intellectual chord in you.

Reading religious scripture, literature, or poetry can be a source of tremendous healing. There is something about the beauty of words placed powerfully together on a page that can enter deep into our unconscious and become part of us. Norman Vincent Peale, writing in the Christian tradition, knew this. He often counseled people to keep a card with a Bible passage on it, and to read it over and over and commit it to memory. Then they could turn to the words inside themselves, like a secret mantra, to find strength in difficult times. As a teenager, I memorized the long mantra from Frank Herbert's *Dune* that begins "I shall not fear, fear is the mind killer, fear is the little death." Despite its unlikely source, those words were, as they are today, a deeply satisfying way to find my center when I feel overwhelmed.

The quote you chose today, no matter where it originated, bears an invitation to weave its message into the warp of your life. Take a moment to reflect on why you chose these words. Consider committing to memory a piece of poetry, a scriptural passage, or a few words from a piece of fiction that moves you. Words can become lifetime friends, as well as lifelines in difficult times.

Verbal Prayer

Consider why you are drawn to certain words or pieces of literature. Is there a mystical aspect in yourself that recognizes the power of certain collections of words? Do the words you have selected today simply capture or mirror what you already feel and know to be true within yourself? Or do they point to a kind of undiscovered country—a place or idea that you sense is broader than your current way of thinking? Do your words support or challenge you? Excite or comfort you? Find a way to give thanks for the gift of the written word. Read aloud to someone else a passage that moves you, sharing your love of language, and listen carefully as the person in turn shares a personal perspective on what you have read. Write about the experience in your journal.

Today spend ten minutes on centering prayer.

DAY FOUR

> I was all alone, and those people were screaming, and suddenly I saw God smiling and I smiled. A woman was standing there, near the school door, and she shouted at me, "Hey you little nigger, what you smiling at?" I looked right at her face and I said, "At God." Then she looked up at the sky and then she looked at me, and she didn't call me any more names.
>
> Robert Coles, *The Spiritual Life of Children*

Contemplation

Find a picture of yourself as a child or draw one. Look closely at the little being that you once were. Can you see echoes of that child in the adult you are now—the fears, the triumphs, the little scars, and the new-summer-sneaker joys? How do those etchings express themselves? In your gift for play? In your fears? What do you feel as you look at this child? How has your awareness of both yourself and the world changed? Write down what you might say to your younger self, now that you have grown older and wiser. Write down what your younger self might say to you!

Verbal Prayer

Say aloud your memories of childhood, both good and bad, and know that the child within is listening for the truth of those words. What aspects of your childhood do you want to release? What aspects do you wish to cherish and honor? What do these poles of cherishing and releasing say to you about the person you are today? Ask yourself how you might use the echoes of yourself as a child to bring a sense of play to your adult life, or to encourage the gift of empathy when working with children. What ways are you called to reach out to the children in your life?

Today spend ten minutes on centering prayer.

DAY FIVE

> What is to reach the heart must come from above, if it does not come thence, it will be nothing but notes—body without spirit.
>
> Marion Scotts, *Beethoven*

Contemplation

Music has a particular power, awe, and majesty. Sometimes it is like the sound the sun might make as it bounces off golden autumn leaves. Other times, music captures the deep swell of the wind pushing the waves of a lake into a white froth, only to fall quiet, secretive, and small, like the emerging butterfly sliding from its dry husk of a cocoon. Good music, whether it makes use of lyrics or not, becomes a kind of poetry—an intimate conversation in a language that transcends words. Today, pick a favorite piece of music, and really listen to that conversation. If you don't have a tape deck or CD player, turn on the radio and let a new song introduce itself to you. Give yourself to the moment, and really listen as the sound unfolds.

Verbal Prayer

Offer a verbal thanks for the gift of music in whatever way appeals to you. Maybe sing your offering! Consider how the many forms of music might be seen as an aspect of divine creativity. Share with another how music affects (or doesn't affect) you own life. Consider some of the following questions in your journal: Do you think music might be seen as conversation and communication? Does this concept suggest new ways to communicate with God or others? Are you able to feel the presence of God in music? Why or why not?

Today spend ten minutes on centering prayer.

DAY SIX

> To foster compassion within ourselves also fosters tolerance—the recognition and acceptance of our inability to control all that life brings our way. When we understand that feeling pain, sorrow, loss, disappointment, greed, anger, envy and fear are inevitable elements of human experience, it is easier to be in the presence of these feelings without criticizing those—including ourselves—who express them.
>
> Nancy J. Napier, *Sacred Practices for Conscious Living*

Contemplation

Dig out a hand mirror, or move into a restroom or bedroom where you have access to a large wall mirror. Now take a few minutes to look deeply at yourself. This is not an exercise to discover new wrinkles or bemoan your oily skin or your bald patch! Instead, really see yourself there—the way you smile, what happens when you frown, the color of your eyes, the shape of your ears. Now look for a moment into your own eyes, as you might look into the eyes of someone you love. Feel compassion for this face. As countless religious leaders have said down through the centuries, compassion for others begins with having compassion for ourselves. The Tibetan Buddhist practice of Tonglen, for instance, asks practitioners to breathe in the pieces of themselves that are dark, hurting, and tender and to breathe out compassion, acceptance, and peace. In that dynamic exchange, students of Tibetan Buddhism begin to understand that they are capable of a loving kindness that can echo in their interactions with others, breath by mindful breath.

Verbal Prayer

Speak out loud how you honestly feel about your body. Watch yourself in the mirror as you say the words that come to mind. Are they hurtful? Supportive and compassionate? Where have the roots of your bodily perception come from? In your journal, write about how messages we have received from others and from the media have affected what we see in a mirror. If you are angry or upset by what you see when you look in the mirror, frame your anger or fear or sadness in the form of a prayer of lament. How might we use our own pain or peaceful joy about our body as a way to relate to others with compassion?

Today spend ten minutes on centering prayer.

Week Two

DAY ONE

> Strain every nerve in every possible way to know and experience yourself as you really are. It will not be long, I suspect, before you have a real knowledge and experience of God as He is.
>
> Anonymous, *The Cloud of Unknowing*

Contemplation

Move to the center of the room or space in which you are working. Give yourself a lot of personal space. Take off your shoes and socks, and spread your toes wide across the floor so that you feel stable and grounded. Lift up through the front of your thighs, imagining that your legs go all the way up to your armpits. Move your elbows slightly away from your body, let your hands fall naturally, and feel the entire length of your arms all the way into your fingertips. Your head should feel like it is floating gently atop your spine, and your chin will pull in just a bit, lengthening the back of the neck. Hold this position with smooth breathing, letting tension leak away. As you simply stand there, feel the floor beneath your feet, and follow the breath as it moves in and out of your lungs. Is it hard to stay balanced? Are your thoughts scattered or focused? Are you aware of any pain or stiffness? Do any strong emotions come to the surface as you stand there? So often we feel the need to move, to be doing something. Today, just stand there for a few minutes and feel what it is like to be instead of always doing.

Verbal Prayer

Sit down with your journal and explore the ways might you bring the experience of be-ing into your life? For example, could you just sit out in your backyard for a few minutes a day, or pause to watch a squirrel cavort along a sidewalk as you walk to your workplace? How are such interludes at least potentially healing? What emotions or thoughts arise within you as you pause during your day? Can these movements of the mind in turn become touchstones for your growing self awareness, even if they don't always bring tranquility? Invoke the names of God that are associated with be-ing, such as *Tao*, and *Great Mother*. How does the God of timelessness, dynamic stillness, and wide-open spaces feel to you?

Today, try to increase your centering prayer experience to fifteen minutes.

DAY TWO

> The first thing contemplation is not is a relaxation exercise!
>
> Thomas Keating, *Open Mind, Open Heart*

Contemplation

Contemplation, as expressed by Thomas Keating, is more about being exquisitely awake than relaxed and distanced from the world. Awareness is a powerful ally to personal health, because being awake encourages us to be conscious and to take responsibility for all aspects of our well-being, including what we put into our mouths and bodies. Whether facing the brightly lit aisles of the supermarket or an enticing menu, we are called to practice a mindful awareness of what we are purchasing. Educating ourselves about nutrition and the effects of our agricultural methods on our environment is one way to begin waking up to what we eat. In other words, our contemplation practice flows off the chair and into the world.

Today, begin simply by reading the ingredients of one item you recently purchased from the grocery. Do you recognize all the ingredients that go into the product you are holding? Do you know if any of it is bad for your health? Write in your journal all the words you don't know at first glance, and spend some time with a dictionary or in a library looking them up. Were you surprised by what you found in your food? Do you feel differently about the food you purchased? Are you willing to learn more? Far from chaining us to another set of things to worry about, educating ourselves about what we consume is an act of responsibility and self-knowledge. By understanding a little bit about nutrition, we place ourselves in the position to make wise, healthy choices. Such choices, day to day, become part of the daily fabric of our lives; indeed, food is one of the most basic strands of that weave.

Verbal Prayer

Visit with someone (or talk to yourself) about how hard or easy it is to own the food choices you make. If this is an area of your life where you feel competent, think about what led you to your current eating style. How might you gently and compassionately share your knowledge with others, including children? In what way does your selection of food connect with your understanding of the divine? How does the idea of mindful or prayerful food selection sit with you?

Today spend fifteen minutes on centering prayer.

DAY THREE

> We receive fragments of holiness, glimpses of eternity, brief moments of insight. Let us gather them up for the precious gifts that they are and renewed by their grace, move boldly into the unknown.
>
> Sara Moores Campbell, "Benediction"

Contemplation

Today, quote from one of your favorite songs. It can be quite simple—just a few lines that you easily recall. Song lyrics have a way of worming themselves deeply into our subconscious, appearing when we least expect them. My mother commented the other day that hymns from her childhood have been paying her a visit lately, popping into her head at odd moments throughout the day. Some teachers use rhyming poetry and musical tunes to help their students remember facts more readily. And all of us have had the experience of hearing a song that we just couldn't get out of our heads. In a way, a song has the capacity to become a kind of prayer. The words, playing through our minds, can help us to slow the churning of worrisome thoughts or endless cycles of guilt or fear. Sometimes lyrics speak clearly and deeply to a specific pain or joy we are experiencing. For some of us, a song can provide a touchstone for our faith and an affirmation of our daily lives. Today, speculate in your journal about why the words you chose have wormed their way into your life. When did you first hear this song? Do its words evoke memories of a special, or perhaps difficult, time? Do the words themselves carry a special message or meaning that you have taken to heart?

Verbal Prayer

Share the lyrics of your song with a friend, and ask if your friend, too, can find a few words that have become part of his or her consciousness. Are the lyrics of the two songs in any way connected? Can you see more of your friend when he or she shares these special lyrics? How do you feel about connecting with the divine through song? Can song become another prayer form in and of itself? If this exercise left you vaguely distressed because no song lyrics readily came to mind, ask yourself how you usually learn. Perhaps you are strongly visual or hearing impaired, and sound of any kind doesn't hold a lot of meaning for you. How does that make you feel when you are invited into music at a worship service, or even a party? Does this affect your faith journey in positive or negative ways?

Today spend fifteen minutes on centering prayer.

DAY FOUR

> The work of healing is in peeling away the barriers of fear and past conditioning that keep us unaware of our true nature of wholeness and love.
>
> Joan Borysenko, *Minding the Body, Mending the Mind*

Contemplation

We can bring a sense of personal intention to the act of healing the hurts of the body, emotions, or spirit. I don't believe this to mean that we can somehow magically "fix" ourselves by some kind of right thinking, prayer discipline, diet, or artistic expression. I believe such creative responses work together like laced fingers beneath a heavy load to support the doctor's medicine or the counselor's words. One of my favorite ways of using intention is to pick up a pen and start doodling. Sometimes, simply expressing my hurt or fear though drawing can help begin the process of healing. Pictures don't require words or coherent thoughts. Like songs, pictures can potentially serve as a vehicle for self-expression and help us yield to something of beauty and insight that is within us.

Today, collect some colored pens, crayons, or whatever drawing materials you have on hand. Now, sit for a moment and think about where you could use some kind of healing in your life. Maybe there is an old emotional wound from childhood, when the other kids teased you and called you "Fattie." Or perhaps an old broken bone aches a lot in the winter, and you want a way to focus on it and accept its message. Maybe you feel a pain in your spirit from a time when you were not allowed to speak your truth to a loved one or your parents. Sit quietly with your eyes shut, and allow an image to come to you that expresses the concept "healing." Don't worry if the picture seems to have nothing to do with the issue you have raised. It might be free-form or very small and detailed. Be aware of the shades that are forming in your mind and what objects arise. Do they carry any meaning for you? How does the forming mental picture make you feel? Now, try to express this image in a drawing as best you can. Don't worry; no one will see this work of your hand and heart unless you choose to share it. Take some time to sit with the picture after you have drawn it, and if you are so moved, write about your experience in your journal.

Verbal Prayer

Consider how God and creativity dance together. What part does imagery play in your understanding of the divine? Visit with someone, or with yourself, about the things you found difficult about this exercise. Maybe nothing visual came to mind, or when you tried to capture the vision, the colors or shapes wouldn't cooperate. What does this say to you about imagination and about personal compassion? Does it seem strange to connect imagery and drawing with a sense of healing? What did you draw when you were a child? What was your favorite color? How can shared art create a sense of community among people? Is shared art capable of moving us to a different level of healing? What can you do to promote such exchanges among people?

Today spend fifteen minutes on centering prayer.

DAY FIVE

> My sisters in Christ will learn by doing. They will sing eight offices a day without fail, and the order and the design will begin to emerge for them from the dailyness of the singing. . . . It is clear that music—singing the offices and listening to the sacred texts, even adding some new music of my own—is my best hope for teaching.
>
> Barbara Lachman, *The Journal of Hildegard of Bingen*

Contemplation

Put on a piece of classical music, or tune into your local public radio station if you don't own any classical music recordings. What moods does the music evoke? How does your body feel if the music triggers emotions? I have learned that certain kinds of classical music make studying easier (for example, the Baroque masters Vivaldi, Corelli, and Albinoni), while the stirring music of Tchaikovsky tends to make me vaguely unsettled and energetic. How are you feeling the music you have selected? What emotions arise? What physiological responses can you tune into? What thoughts or images begin to impinge on your consciousness? Is a story or poem being born as you listen? Or can you feel a soft dis-ease with the music in yourself? Can you use this awareness of the connection between musical compositions and your own bodily responses in a way that could promote healing, help calm frayed nerves, frame a time of change in your life, or encourage creativity? Take time to write the name of the piece you are listening to in your journal, and remark about your reaction to it.

Verbal Prayer

How do you use music to connect with the divine? Does an appreciation of music come in through your head, through your heart, or through a body moving with the rhythms and tones? What does that say to you about yourself? Why don't all people respond on the same level to a given piece of music? How can music both link and separate people? Consider the impact of sound on mind, body, and spirit. How does the music feel different from the loud truck outside your window or the television commercial?

Today spend fifteen minutes on centering prayer.

DAY SIX

> Beauty is merely the spiritual making itself known sensuously.
>
> G.W.F. Hegel, "The Philosophy of Religion"

Contemplation

Autumn is the time when the leaves come down to us, each one unique and wholly its own. This one is brilliant red, almost painfully perfect and balanced. This one is covered with dark spots from some earlier sickness. Green and yellow swirl through another leaf, as if it couldn't quite make up its mind what color suited it best. They have all launched into a moment of wind-ballet grace, only to end up here on our sidewalks and rambling driveways, a glorious flat bouquet that softens the lines of cement and crinkles the air as you pass. Today, no matter what season you find yourself in, take a moment to closely examine a leaf. Trace its veins, smell its skin, think a moment about its life path. Reflect on the following questions in your journal: What parts of yourself are glorious? What parts have unsightly little spots, and how do you feel about them? What leaves within you need to fall from the tree, to make room for the buds of spring? How are you like the leaves on a vast world tree?

Verbal Prayer

How do the textures and colors of a single leaf make you feel? Think about that individual leaf as part of the cycle of life going on all around us. How does this leaf, that interesting pebble, or this raindrop call you back to God? Did you experience a sense of stewardship for the life of this planet as you held the leaf? Or if this experience left you cold, consider why.

Today spend fifteen minutes on centering prayer.

Week Three

DAY ONE

> Afoot and light-hearted, I take to
> The open road,
> Healthy, free, the world before me.
>
> Henceforth, I ask not good fortune—
> I myself am good fortune:
> Strong and content,
> I travel the open road.
>
> Walt Whitman, "Song of the Open Road"

Contemplation

For some people, sitting meditation can be the best way to reach the inner calm and clarity that presages wisdom. But for others, the rhythm of walking, the feeling of their feet on the ground, the beat of their heart, and the soft intakes of breath help them find their center. Mindful walking, which simply means being fully present in the act of walking, is a powerful way to reach a state of relaxation and awareness. Take a walk around your living room, or out on your sidewalk, or through the woods that wait beyond your back step. See what it feels like when you are fully aware of the experience of walking. How does your body feel? Do thoughts intrude quite as easily when you focus on the swing of your arms, the texture of the carpet or ground, the little shifts your body must make to keep you mobile and upright? Take a moment when you return from your walk, and note what you discovered in your journal.

Verbal Prayer

Contemplate how it felt to be aware of the mechanics of your own movement outside or within your home. How do you think others feel about the simple act of walking? Pray for those who find movement difficult or even impossible; allow yourself to experience their world in your imagination. How might mindful walking, in companionship with another or others, be a healing experience? Is there a way to bring the consciousness of mindful walking to all physical activities in your life? Why might you resist such a practice? What might be its gifts? How does mindfulness facilitated by movement help you connect with God?

Try extending your centering prayer practice to twenty minutes this week.

DAY TWO

> Is it oblivion or absorption, Emily Dickinson asks, when we forget? When some new thought, feeling, or notion presents itself, we can't forget it or overlook it. When we have invited it in or agreed to live in its company, maybe then it won't be such a preoccupation. It will be forgotten—not exiled into oblivion, but absorbed into being.
>
> Thomas Moore, *Meditations*

Contemplation

The challenge is this: Faced with more and more research that shows a diet heavy in meats and dairy products contributes to heart disease and to many forms of cancer, how do we consciously make necessary changes in our diets? And why is it often so hard to do so? When we talk about looking seriously at our diet, we are also looking seriously at our eating habits. What and how we eat are learned behaviors, just as changing what we eat is also a learning process. When I was a child, I learned that if I took in just a little bit of information at a time, the new facts stuck better. So I would study only half of my spelling list one day, and add the other half the next day. Lifestyle changes work the same way. Today, challenge yourself to find one easy low-fat or vegetarian recipe to try sometime during the week. That's all—just one new dish. Next week, try another recipe. Keep the ones you like in a little notebook that you can easily refer to. Over the course of a couple months, you will begin to have a collection of recipes that are kinder to your health. And you won't feel stressed out by a radical change in your dietary habits. Sometime, come back to your journal, and talk about your new adventures in cooking and how it feels to integrate new habits into your being.

Verbal Prayer

How do you feel about food and the habits you have built up around food? Do you experience any resistance to change when looking at new recipes or new diets? How does that very resistance feel to you? What are its roots? How does a prayer practice or being mindful help you support change? What are the complex interactions between socioeconomic status and healthy heating? Between gender and food? Between race and food? How might eating a healthy diet or helping someone else learn to make good choices be a kind of prayer practice?

Today spend twenty minutes on centering prayer.

DAY THREE

> Why should we live in such a hurry and waste of life? We are determined to be starved before we are hungry. I wish to live deliberately, to front only the essential facts of life. I wish to learn what life has to teach, and not, when I come to die, discover that I have not lived....
>
> Henry David Thoreau, "To Live Deliberately"

Contemplation

I have always been amazed at the power the television and the theater can exert. They can affect our mood, inform and misinform us, manipulate us into buying things we don't want or need, or uplift us by whisking us off to foreign lands or into the wonders of the ocean depths. Like all things of power in this life, the media have the potential to be a healing force or a force that contributes to our daily stress. In what ways have TV and cinema productions uplifted you? Have you also felt abused or numbed by what you chose to watch? How do you make informed viewing choices for yourself or your children? Has TV become your drug of choice, keeping you from the real fabric of life?

Take the initiative today, and simply turn the TV off. In your journal, reflect on ways you might fill the space left by the silent television. Consider what programs are important to you, and why. Challenge yourself to have television-free days during the week.

Verbal Prayer

Pray about the role of the media in your life, and whether it is a healthy and uplifting element. Speak out loud about what you like and dislike about television or the cinema. What resistance did you feel when you were asked to turn your TV off? (Be careful to speak about emotions as well as thoughts.) On what levels do the media and the divine connect? Is there a valid connection between the media and a conscious understanding and stewardship of our society? Can watching television or movies ever be a form of prayer? Thank God for the presence of technology in our lives, and ask for the wisdom to use it wisely.

Today spend twenty minutes on centering prayer.

DAY SIX

> But the world is not immune to change. On the contrary, it is the nature of all things to change. Look at our lives, how they move and shift: Once we were young, and now we are older, friends and family have come and gone, social circles have evolved, jobs have changed, we may have moved our homes many times. What we once loved may have faded or passed away; what we now love, how long will that last? And what will arise to take its place as we walk the path of our life?
>
> Wayne Muller, *Legacy of the Heart*

Contemplation

"Find a penny, pick it up. All day long, you'll have good luck." Although we may outgrow this childhood game, a variation called "penny meditation" may help us keep in touch with the passage of time. When you find a penny lying on the sidewalk, or in the parking lot, or on floor of your closet, pick it up and check the date. Then try to remember what was going on at that time in your life. This little exercise can help get you thinking about how you have changed, how your life is different from year to year, how the memories of important events or mundane stretches of time sketch a portrait of who you are. It can also call you back to the present, because you may find you are always on the lookout for that penny in your path! Try this little exercise sometime, or invent another way of looking back at the changes in your life. For now, instead of hunting for a penny, pull a coin out of your purse or pocket, and examine the date. Then spend some time with your journal, reminiscing about that particular time in the history of you.

Verbal Prayer

Pray about how you feel about the passage of time. Share with yourself or someone close to you any fears about looking back, and why those fears might be arising in you. Consider what hands may have held your coin and why it ended up where it did. Is it possible to see the flow of life in even a little piece of metal? What might you have remembered about the date on your coin if you had found it four years ago? Ten years ago? Yesterday? How does your understanding of the divine jibe with an experience of yourself as a being moving through time? Look again at your coin's date. How was your image of God different then? Or has it stayed much the same?

Today spend twenty minutes on centering prayer.

Week Four

DAY ONE

> Touch means contact—the relationship with what lies outside our own periphery, the ground beneath our feet. And for humans, as for other animals, touch is of vital importance. It gives reassurance, warmth, pleasure, comfort and renewed vitality. It tells us we are not alone.
>
> Lucinda Lidell, *The Book of Massage*

Contemplation

First, find and light a candle. Then, very carefully, cup your hands around the flame. Can you feel the warmth, the small draft of air pushed upward by the heat? If you don't have access to a candle, run your hands under hot water for a few minutes, or hold your hands over a hot-air vent to warm them. Then place them where you feel any kind of discomfort: on your sore elbows; on the shoulder that catches a little; or against your heart, where you feel sadness or anger. Sometimes the simple gesture of touch, even when that touch originates and ends with ourselves, can be deeply healing. It can also be a conduit for communicating our love. My fourteen-year-old son still asks to have his back rubbed, particularly when he has had a rough day at school. It makes him feel cared about, and my touch reassures him that he is loved. The simple trust that comes with allowing a loving touch, and in turn touching in love, can be a revelation and the discovery of the physical embodiment of spirit.

Verbal Prayer

Bring your concerns about touch into a prayer, sharing any fear or anger that touch brings up for you. Think about the ways touch can heal or hurt, and write a short poem or draw a picture about those thoughts. How is the divine manifest through the physical for you? If you have been ill, how might knowledgeable touch, such as massage or some other medium, be used to support your healing process? Send a prayer to children who do not receive a loving sense of touch from the adults around them.

Today spend twenty-five minutes on centering prayer.

DAY TWO

> We must not be thinking of food all twenty-four hours the day. The only thing needful is perpetual vigilance, which will help us find out soon when we eat for self-indulgence and when in order only to sustain the body.
>
> Mohandas Gandhi, *Vows and Observances*

Contemplation

Here in America, we are surrounded by so much plenty. Most people have access to all the varieties of food they could want. The water we drink, in most cases, is fairly clean. And yet many of our diseases take root in poor dietary choices. As a nation, we are overweight. It makes me wonder if what we thirst for is something that material food and water cannot really satisfy. Today, I ask you to contemplate this in your journal. Then, if you are so moved, set aside a day this week to undertake a fast on bread and water. The technique is quite simple. Instead of a complex breakfast, lunch, and dinner, simply have a slice of whole-grain bread (without lots of butter, please!), and drink about eight glasses of water throughout the day. Be sure to pick out a loaf that is made without preservatives or lots of added sugars and fats. Or consider baking a whole-grain loaf yourself the night before your fast. The act of mixing and kneading your own bread and then watching it rise and bake is in itself a spiritual experience! On the day of your fast, go slowly. Take plenty of time to read and pray. In a place of emptiness, perhaps we can begin to hear the word of God more and the word of the candy bar less.

Verbal Prayer

Pray about what you hunger for in your life, and how these hungers may result in making poor food choices. Seriously consider the idea of a fast: What scares you about the exercise? What excites you? Pray about the experience of plenty in your life—the variety of food and drink we have access to. Do you believe fasting makes room for the divine? Or do you feel it is like a mortification of the body, and thus strays off a balanced path?

Today spend twenty-five minutes on centering prayer.

DAY THREE

> We have a great deal more kindness than is ever spoken.
> The whole human family is bathed with an element of love like a fine ether.
>
> Ralph Waldo Emerson, "The Heart Knoweth"

Contemplation

Have you ever had the experience of thinking about someone, and suddenly he or she is on the phone or has sent you an e-mail? What is this magic that keeps us connected, even when the miles separate us from family and friends, and even when we fall into bed so tired from the day's activities that we fall immediately to sleep? Partially, the alchemy must come from two souls caring for each other, two minds recognizing the gentle bonds that they share. Today, I challenge you to contact someone who is important in your life, either by paying a visit, picking up the phone, or sending an e-mail. Sometimes we get flying along so fast that we begin to lose touch with the people who enrich our lives. Spend some time with your journal, talking a bit about the role all relationships play in the expression and understanding of your spiritual journey.

Verbal Prayer

Pray about the people who have been missing from your life. Imagine you can touch their hearts, one by one, as they come up in your consciousness. Notice and pray about any resistance you have to reaching out to certain people. Seek an inner guidance about what can be done to address it. Write a poem or draw a picture about the importance of friendships in your life, thanking God for these gifts. Craft a lament for the passage of friendships and relationships.

Today spend twenty-five minutes on centering prayer.

DAY FOUR

> The divine nature, free and perfect and blissful, must be manifested in the individual in order that it may manifest in the world.
>
> Sri Aurobindo, *Synthesis of Yoga*

Contemplation

Today, gather together your drawing materials. Close your eyes, and ask that a representation of your relationship with God be sketched on your inner eye. Be patient. You may have to sit still for many minutes until the impression becomes really tangible. Perhaps you will see only colors, or maybe an abstract symbol will present itself to you. Or you may find a picture forming of a safe place you have been or a memory of standing in a beautiful spot. Once you are able to hold this image, slowly open your eyes and sketch what you experienced. Be as abstract or as concrete as you wish; this picture is only for you, to remind yourself of your connection with the divine.

Verbal Prayer

Pray about what meaning your symbol has for you. Think about why this particular symbol might have arisen today. Speak aloud your frustrations with this exercise if it was difficult to conceptualize, in symbolic form, your relationship with the divine. Consider other ways you might tangibly connect to your relationship with God, say, through music, touch, movement, or another creative act.

Today spend twenty-five minutes on centering prayer.

DAY FIVE

> Where is God my maker, who giveth songs in the night?
>
> Job 15:10

Contemplation

We are bombarded by sound in this culture. Whether from the roaring sirens, or the insistent prattle of the television, or the voices in the apartment below, our lives are immersed in sound that researchers say contributes to stress. And yet sound can also be a healing presence, sending a message to our nervous system to relax. Today, put on a piece of quiet music as you write in your journal. You can tune in to a radio station that specializes in quiet jazz, or perhaps you own some music CDs that fit the bill. How do these kinds of melodies make you feel? Does their mood affect you, or do you largely ignore them as you write? Do they evoke any images? Do you think that music, of this less strident variety, can be an ally at the end of a stressful day?

Verbal Prayer

Consider all the variety of sounds in your life, focusing on those that seem to make you feel good (for instance, bird calls, wind in the trees, or soft jazz) and those that jar and impose on you. Can sound represent a healing force? How could sound be used constructively with small children? People who are ill? To better frame a dinner? Give voice to the frustrations you encountered in this exercise, trying to be clear about the feelings you have about quiet music.

Today spend twenty-five minutes on centering prayer.

DAY SIX

> For it is not physical solitude that actually separates one from other men, not physical isolation, but spiritual isolation. It is not the desert island nor the stony wilderness that cuts you from the people you love. It is the wilderness in the mind, the desert wastes in the heart through which one wanders lost and a stranger.
>
> Anne Morrow Lindbergh, *Gift from the Sea*

Contemplation

Do you isolate yourself? Do you build up walls of indifference, or fear, or anger? Walls people build between themselves and others have bricks of many different shades. Some seem gray with depression. Others are brittle and orange with fear. Still others are dark brown, hard with past resentment and yesterday's hurts solidified and implacable. To reach out to others, a little bit of our interior walls must come down. I have found that a simple feather pen often can start the process. (A ballpoint pen will serve just as well.) In your journal, write down a list of people you know, and next to each name note one positive aspect of that person. Perhaps you remember the kind word your high school teacher once said, or the way your neighbor always smiles her good morning to you. Spend a moment with each of the names you have written down, seeing the blessings they have brought to your life. When we isolate ourselves, no matter how good our reasons, we miss out on the interconnected web of relationships that both binds and supports us. Modern medicine notes that contact with other human beings can actually strengthen healing responses in people who are ill. Our connection with people, then, is a gift for the mind, the body, and the spirit.

Verbal Prayer

Send a prayer out to each of the people who have been instrumental in your spiritual life, and ask God to bless each of them. Muse about the times when it seemed necessary to shut yourself away from people; share this experience with your journal or someone you trust, and discuss what was going on inside yourself. Craft a poem of joy about the companionship you have experienced on your life journey. Brainstorm ways that you might better open yourself up to new friendships; make a list of possible ways in your journal, and then pick one and act on it!

Today spend twenty-five minutes on centering prayer.

Week Five

DAY ONE

> Trust that by putting your body into different positions, you explore the many levels of being that a human can be confronted with. In doing so, you validate and affirm the very nature of existence. Acceptance is not passivity or giving up. Rather, it is an active willingness to face all aspects of our humanness. Acceptance is an acknowledgment of what is and an opportunity to find meaning in it.
>
> Rachel Schaeffer, *Yoga for Your Spiritual Muscles*

Contemplation

No matter what our age, a little stretching can do us good. Stretching releases tension and encourages mobility and flexibility, which in turn can protect us from injuries if we fall. Think about the word stretch. It can be a prescription not just for the body but for the mind as well. Stretching encourages us to be very present in the moment, feeling how our body is moving and letting go of troublesome thoughts or racing anxiety. Today, gently move your body in stretches that feel comfortable to you. Perhaps gently rotate your neck, or extend your arms out to the side, reaching in each direction. Do what feels natural to you. Breathe slowly and deeply through your nose, and really focus on each movement. (If you are interested in a stretching routine, consult the Resources at the end of this book for a list of good stretching or yoga books.) Write down in your journal the sensations you noted as you stretched. How do you think that the mind, body, and spirit function together as a whole? At what times in your life can you most easily tap into this complex interplay?

Verbal Prayer

Consider at length how stretching brought you (or didn't bring you) into an awareness of the interaction of mind, body, and spirit. How did stretching make you feel, emotionally? Was it frightening? Relaxing? Invigorating? How did your thought processes feel before and after you stretched? Did you feel more clear? More worried about something? How might the feelings of stretch in the body relate to your ability to "stretch" in other areas of your life? Draw a picture about how stretching felt to you.

Today, try to practice your centering prayer for a full half-hour. This manual won't increase the time spent in meditation beyond this point, but if you feel called to pursue this kind of work, please do so!

DAY TWO

> In all societies, both simple and complex, eating is the primary way of initiating and maintaining human relationships. . . . Once the anthropologist finds out where, when and with whom the food is eaten, just about everything else can be inferred about the relations among the society's members. . . . To know what, where, how, when, and with whom people eat is to know the character of their society.
>
> Peter Farb and George Armelagos, *Consuming Passions*

Contemplation

One little rule from my childhood that I have tried to maintain in my own house is that the evening meal is a sit-down affair, without the distraction of the television. Of course, we don't always manage this, but the trick is to aim for frequency rather than rigidity. I like the conversation around the table, the catching up on the day's events, the shared time together. This simple act of eating together can also be a gift that can be shared. Today, I want you to think about offering the present of a shared meal to someone you know or would like to know. Perhaps in the future you will choose to sit down for a candle-lit dinner with your spouse, invite a neighbor over for dinner, or bake a couple loaves of bread that you could share with some new friends at a nursing home. There are so many ways to extend the family table to those who would appreciate the effort and the companionship. In your journal, write a bit about how your family meal is structured, and compare it with the meals you remember from childhood. Are there things you would like to do differently? Are at least some of your mealtime habits nurturing and special? How might you extend your family meal to include others?

Verbal Prayer

Think about how mealtimes are sacred (or not sacred) times for you. Write a bit about sitting down to a rushed fast-food lunch as compared with participating in a more formal dinner. How are the experiences alike? How are they different? Hold in your consciousness any pain that tended to surface around the family table when you were a child. Pray about the ways you might make mealtimes more sacred, even if you are eating off paper and drinking through a plastic straw. How does your prayer life touch your experience of eating?

Today spend thirty minutes on centering prayer.

DAY THREE

> The total absence of humor renders life impossible.
>
> Colette, *Chance Acquaintances*

Contemplation

Humor has been labeled one of the best medicines. And that means it doesn't just treat the body, even though research has shown that laughter may help the immune response; humor has the capacity to heal our spirits as well. Try this little experiment. First, pull your face down into a frown. Hold it there a few minutes. How does it feel? What emotions move through your body? Now, smile! Does your body feel different? Can you describe the difference between a smile and a frown in terms of larger feelings within you? In your journal, think about how you could apply the fine medicine of humor to your physical or emotional self. Perhaps you could make a list of humor resources. Include comedians, funny books, and videos that make you giggle. Then, you will always have a ready-made self-prescription for laughter—and well-being.

Verbal Prayer

Consider what makes you smile and laugh. How do you feel when you've gone a long period without humor or lightheartedness in your life? Talk a little bit about what you think about a prescription for humor: Does actively seeking to tickle our own funny bones seem artificial or contrived? Or does the practice make a lot of sense to you? How do you feel about humor being part and parcel of the divine? Send out a prayer of blessing for someone who always is quick with a joke, or who just has an innate capacity to make you smile.

Today spend thirty minutes on centering prayer.

DAY FOUR

> Love is never abstract. It does not adhere to the universe of the planet or the nation or the institution or the profession, but to the singular sparrows of the street, the lilies of the field, the least of my brethren. Love is not, by its own desire, heroic. It is heroic only when compelled to be. It exists by its willingness to be anonymous, humble and unrewarded.
>
> Wendell Berry, "Word and Flesh"

Contemplation

Gather together your drawing materials. Sit quietly for a moment, and hold the word love in your mind. After a few minutes, watch for a symbol, picture, or color that you associate with the abstract word love. You may find that a great many pictures, symbols, or colors come to mind. Love is not so simple, after all. Open your eyes, and try to capture the essence of love in your journal. Perhaps you will find that a collage of images works best, or maybe something simple captures the spirit of the word. Spend some time with your journal, exploring what that particular representation means to you.

Verbal Prayer

Write a poem or short essay about the image you have drawn today, sharing the insights and revelations that came to you. Pray about your resistance to working on this exercise, and where that resistance might have come from. Consider all the different ways you see love operating in your life. Lament in the form of a song or prayer about the places in your life or the world where you see love absent. Send out a healing prayer of love to someone close to you or who you feel needs this special kind of energy today.

Today spend thirty minutes on centering prayer.

DAY FIVE

> To every thing there is a season and a time to every purpose under heaven . . . a time to weep and a time to laugh; a time to mourn and a time to dance.
>
> Ecclesiastes 3:1, 4

Contemplation

Today, choose a favorite piece of rock and roll, bluegrass, or big band music. The main thing is to find something that makes you tap your foot and puts a bounce into your stride. Your challenge: Move with the music! Get up and dance! (Gently, please, if you haven't been active for a while.) Or stay seated, and move your arms and shoulders with the beat. Tap your foot; snap your fingers. Feel the music moving you. How does this affect your emotional state? Do you find yourself smiling? How does the physical exercise feel? Could music help make walking or running the vacuum cleaner more enjoyable, or would you find it a hindrance? Write about the act of moving to the music in your journal, and see what insights you have gained.

Verbal Prayer

Think about the experience of moving to music, particularly how it applies to feeling alive and dancing with the divine. Pray about some of your reservations about dancing. Write a poem or draw a picture that captures how certain seasons of your life were more or less full with dance, and what the presence or absence of dance has meant to you. Speak aloud about the times you have watched others dance, whether it was at the ballet, at a wedding, or in a makeshift little dance hall in your basement. How did those times feel to you? What made them memorable?

Today spend thirty minutes on centering prayer.

DAY SIX

> Living our lives between the briefness of the daylight and the dark. Kindred in this, each lighted by the same precarious, flickering flame of life, how does it happen that we are not kindred in all things else?
>
> A. Powell Davies, "Strange and Foolish Walls"

Contemplation

Have you ever seen a full-sized Zen rock garden? Imagine an area the size of a large swimming pool, filled with coarse gravel that has been raked each day into patterns that ripple like water. Rising up from that ocean of pebbles and sand, three or four gray boulders sit motionless and timeless. These giants are connected by the gravel, the very ground of their being, yet seemingly wholly apart. When do we, too, hold this kind of deep peace—so still, so patient? When do we feel lonely and apart? What is that grace that sometimes allows us to practice "being" in the bitterest winter or in the summer heat that melts us all? In your journal, contemplate how you are like a great stone embraced by the carefully raked gravel of the world, held by the divine dirt of life that supports and unites us all.

Verbal Prayer

Think about a time you saw a rock that captured your imagination. Why has the memory stayed with you? Consider why you find it difficult or easy to construct analogies between yourself and the natural world. Share with your journal or with some special other the ways that you fit into your life like a boulder snuggled into the gravel. Then talk about the ways you feel isolated. If you have an altar, consider adding a stone that has some kind of meaning for you. Send out a soft prayer to someone who seems to be hunkering, isolated, or hard today.

Today spend thirty minutes on centering prayer.

Week Six

DAY ONE

> Renew thyself completely each day; do it again and again, and forever again.
>
> Chinese inscription cited by Henry David Thoreau in *Walden*

Contemplation

Go into your kitchen and bring back your favorite teacup, coffee mug, or glass. Take a moment to really look at this object. Feel its weight in your hands; trace its lines or decorations as if seeing them for the first time. When did you first purchase your cup? Was it a gift perhaps, symbolizing an important event in your life? How does it feel when you curve your hands around it? Would you miss it if it were damaged beyond repair? Why or why not? See if you can find the simple beauty in a teacup or coffee mug. Things in our lives can become commonplace if we don't slow ourselves down enough to really look. My challenge to you is to notice this simple cup each time you use it this week. Can you continue to see it anew each time? Write a few lines in your journal about the experience.

Verbal Prayer

Write or speak a bit about the beauty in other ordinary objects around you. Does noticing even simple beauty make your day more clear and meaningful? Why or why not? Draw a cartoon about the phenomenon of yard sales or garage sales, where everyone in a neighborhood can find treasures and beauty in other people's junk. Pray about other ways you can enter into the holy present moments of your life.

Today spend thirty minutes on centering prayer.

DAY TWO

> Our consciousness . . . is like a great river on the surface of which our superficial thoughts and experiences are moving by like boats, debris, water skiers or other things. The river itself is the participation God has given us in His own being. It is that part of us on which all the other faculties rest, but we are ordinarily unaware of it because we are absorbed with what is passing by on the surface of the river.
>
> Thomas Keating, *Open Mind, Open Heart*

Contemplation

Water is more than a metaphor for the divine; it is also a very tangible part of our physical life, making it a natural symbol for expressing the rhythms of our spiritual dance. At the same time, we tend to take this natural resource for granted. We simply go to the sink, turn on the faucet, and poof! We have one lovely, sparkling drink. Yet despite its availability, we don't drink enough water. Recommended amounts vary but usually fall around eight glasses each day. It's also important to know that even with our municipal water systems and private wells, our water can contain small amounts of toxic material that, over time, may injure our health. It is worth having your water tested or investing in a simple water purification system for your house. If you are on a tight budget, the pitcher-style water filtration units that can be found at your local department store do a pretty good job of purifying drinking water. One of the kindest things you can do for yourself is to try to drink clean water more often. Perhaps you can say a short prayer of thankfulness each time you take a drink of water. Today, in your journal, think about the miracle of water and how you might increase the amount you drink each day.

Verbal Prayer

Muse about the symbolism of water in your religious tradition or in your understanding of God. How easy or difficult is it to remain conscious of even a simple thing like drinking? Why do you think that this is so? Pray about the image of the boat on the water used in Keating's quote above. Has this been a good metaphor for what you have experienced in your practice of centering prayer?

Today spend thirty minutes on centering prayer.

DAY THREE

All creatures bend to rules, even the stars constrained.

Margaret Starkey, "One Small Face"

Contemplation

Many people—especially young people—think they have no limits. They're quite sure that given enough time, enough information, and enough energy, they can accomplish whatever they set out to do. Yet life—school, work, marriage, personal injuries, family illnesses—usually intervenes to teach us that we do indeed have limits. This knowledge, though, can bring a kind of grace to our lives. I have learned a lot from my limits about what I value, about how to "let go and let God," and about how to ask for help and how to say no in a way that is caring and sincere. Today, write in your journal about the limits you have found in yourself and how those limits might also be seen as blessings in disguise. What have they taught you about yourself?

Verbal Prayer

Consider how limits might enrich your spiritual journey. Muse about the energy you are able to give to different aspects of your life, and how this allocation of energy has changed with age and life circumstances. Write a little bit about why you don't like the whole idea of limits. Send out a prayer for someone who is having difficulty carving out personal space or who seems overwhelmed because of the inability to say no. Draw a picture that captures the positive or negative sides of recognizing limits.

Today spend thirty minutes on centering prayer.

DAY FOUR

> There is no fear in love; but perfect loves casteth out fear.
>
> 1 John 4:18

Contemplation

Gather together your drawing materials. Today, sit quietly for a few moments, and think of a place where you feel safe, sacred, and whole. The place may be very familiar to you—perhaps a favorite armchair in your own home, or your childhood play nook. Or the place may arise out of your imagination. For instance, perhaps you will picture a place that is a composite of several spots you have visited, with your favorite weather thrown in for good measure. The important thing is to recognize the gentle relaxation that comes over you when you visit this place in your imagination. When you can hold the image fairly well in your mind's eye, take up your drawing materials and sketch out the place you visited in your mind. Take some time to write about how you feel wrapped in the mental picture of your safe place.

Verbal Prayer

How do you feel about creating a safe place in your own mind? Does it feel good, odd, frightening in a way, or irrelevant? Hold in your heart today the name of someone who could use a safe place. Pray about the place you created in your mind or recalled: What specifically makes the place safe or special? Consider any differences in how you felt before you went to your safe place in your mind and how you felt afterward. What ramifications does an internal safe place have for your physical health? For your spiritual life?

Today spend thirty minutes on centering prayer.

DAY FIVE

Music is love in search of a word.

Sidney Lanier, *The Symphony*

Contemplation

Music can be seen as the language of the intent and feelings beneath our common spoken tongue. The past few weeks you have immersed yourself in different kinds of music. Today, I ask you to begin to explore the music within yourself. This exercise is very simple. Take up any book, and place it on your lap. Then gently begin to tap it with your hands, making up a little drum rhythm. Don't worry if you feel like you can't keep a beat. This time is for you! Can you remember when a drum could be the kitchen table, pots and pans, or an empty oatmeal container? Push your limits a bit, varying the beat, playing your "drum" a little harder or a little softer. Try to capture what joy might sound like. Is it a fast, lively beat or a slow, stately tapping? Then see what rhythm fear or sadness might suggest. Write down some of your impressions. What is the nature of your own rhythm as you move through life?

Verbal Prayer

Consider how listening to music differs from actually playing your book-drum. If this exercise didn't excite you very much, consider why. Laugh with another as you recall all the many objects from your childhood that became musical instruments: cardboard oatmeal containers that became decorated drums, glasses filled with water that rang like chimes, the two pencils that tapped out a beat on your math book. How does self-made music connect you with the creative principle of God?

Today spend thirty minutes on centering prayer.

DAY SIX

> In addition to figuring out what your priorities are, it is also helpful to figure out what you don't want in your life anymore. This is a subtle distinction, but it's an important one to make. We allow a lot of mental, emotional and psychological clutter to accumulate in our minds and our lives, blocking our access to inner peace.
>
> Elaine St. James, *Inner Simplicity*

Contemplation

There is a lake outside my window, stilled beneath a heavy blanket of snow. It's very difficult at this time of year to know exactly where the lake begins and where the gentle slope of land ends. Have you ever felt a little like this lake, unsure where your borders should be? Do you trust yourself, or do you allow yourself to be influenced by what other people believe or conceive for you? These are times when you have to warm your inner lake, thaw into a vital flowing body of water with clear, undulating lines between yourself and others. At other times, you may have reveled in feeling like this winter lake, particularly when the strict line between yourself and God dissolves a little during prayer. Our personal limits can protect us or enslave us. Write about the times you need to set limits and the times when the line between yourself and others or God seems to disappear. It is up to us to judge when to be the lake of white, and when to move in a dynamic dance within clear shorelines.

Verbal Prayer

Consider how you have experienced the metaphor of the winter lake and the summer lake. Can you relate at all to this internal shifting of boundaries? Pray about the boundaries you must set in your life in order to be whole and healthy in your mind-body-spirit. Send out a prayer for someone you know who has trouble setting boundaries. Consider when boundaries are helpful and when they might cut you off from being in relationship with others. Write a short story about how children can use the metaphoric dance of the winter and summer lake.

Today spend thirty minutes on centering prayer.

Week Seven

DAY ONE

> Imagination is a good horse to carry you over the ground, not a magic carpet to take you away from the world of possibilities.
>
> Robertson Davies, *The Manticore*

Contemplation

Today, I ask you to find a toy or something you might have played with when you were young. If you have children in your house, your task should be easy. If not, think back to what you would have used for a toy if you were a child visiting the home of friends without children. Perhaps a ball of yarn suggested a rope that could be braided to capture imaginary horses. Or recall that once upon a time, the wooden spoon became a pirate's sword. Take some time to remember how it felt to play. Maybe move the toy car over the carpet, or throw the ball up in the air and catch it. Imagination drove our younger lives, and even though it might be a bit rusty, it is still there within our grasp. Write in your journal how it felt to play for even a few minutes, and consider ways that the adult might learn to imagine for the fun of it, today and every day.

Verbal Prayer

Think about this gift of imagination, and how hard or easy it was to recall an attitude of play. Pray about why you didn't want to do today's exercise; be sure that you don't feel guilty about not wanting to participate! Explore the ways you could play during the day—not necessarily with children's toys but perhaps through a special hobby or by making a picnic to take to the park. Come up with a list of ways you might encourage other adults to play, and then pick one and put it into action!

Today spend thirty minutes on centering prayer.

DAY TWO

> Greater than prayer is the spirit in which it is uttered.
>
> Glenn Clark, "The Soul's Sincere Desire"

Contemplation

Today, in your journal, write down your favorite mealtime prayer. If you don't have one, I encourage you to design your own that you can bring to each meal. A mealtime prayer is a wonderful way to stay in touch with the Spirit at least once a day. The presence of food is a potent reminder of the bounty of the physical world. And by taking a brief moment to pray, providing you don't just rush through it by rote, you enter into a quieter time. Your physiological systems have the chance to downshift, to prepare to process the food you are about to eat. There is also the chance you will enjoy your meal more by staying focused after the prayer. Sometime in the future, write in your journal how it feels to begin each meal with a blessing. If mealtime prayers are already part of your home tradition, you might spend some time writing about how you learned to pray at mealtimes as a child. What is the history of prayer in your family?

Verbal Prayer

Consider how it feels to pray before each meal. How do you see it helping to further your spiritual life? Write or speak frankly about why you don't like participating in mealtime prayers. As you sit down to your meal, consider praying for those in need, who don't have access to good food or water.

Today spend thirty minutes on centering prayer.

DAY THREE

> You see, we never look at life, our own life, as a tremendous movement with a great depth, a vastness. We have reduced life to such a shoddy little affair. And life is really the most sacred thing in existence.
>
> J. Krishnamurti, *This Light in Oneself*

Contemplation

Today, in your journal, write your own quote from anywhere. Perhaps your grandmother had some words of wisdom, or your boss came up with a good line the other day. Perhaps some stanza of poetry or the refrain of a song occurs to you. Maybe you gained insight through a joke your child shared with you, or maybe you read a bumper sticker that hit home. If you can't think of anything, don't worry. You could use this opportunity to turn to a poem or sacred text and let a passage suggest itself to you. When you have your quote, take some time with your journal to explore why you chose these words. What wisdom do they impart that may hint at the greater part of the tree that is "spread out/In the soil under your feet"?

Verbal Prayer

How does it feel to recall words that have meaning? Why do some phrases go so deeply within you? Pray about the impact that words have on your life. Voice any anxiety you experienced when trying to come up with a quote. Consider ways that you could share meaningful quotes with others, perhaps by printing a unique quotations page in your church newsletter or using quotes as headers or postscripts when you write to your friends.

Today spend thirty minutes on centering prayer.

DAY FOUR

> The real message of humor therapy is that we must learn to establish a sense of emotional balance, to feel the range of feelings—anger, fear, joy, love and so on. Shortly before he died, Norman Cousins said that it wasn't humor that healed him; it was love. Humor, he said, was a way in which compassion could do its healing work.
>
> Gordon Edlin, Eric Golanty, and Kelli Brown, *Health and Wellness*

Contemplation

Today, try your hand at a little humor! In your journal, make four boxes on the unlined page. To do this, draw a line right down the center of the page, making two columns. Then draw a line through the middle of the columns. Now, using stick figures if you want, or more fleshed-out characters if you prefer, design your very own comic strip. Maybe you will choose to illustrate a joke; perhaps you will pose a philosophical conundrum or simply show the funny side of your child taking a bath in his Cheerios and milk. The important thing is to come up with something that tickles your funny bone, makes you smile, encourages that little glow of happiness inside you. Then, in your journal, talk about what it is like to recall or even create something funny. How did your body feel? Is your mood any different from when you began the exercise? Do you agree with Norman Cousins that humor may be the way to open up to compassion? Why or why not?

Verbal Prayer

Share your comic strip with someone you love, or post it on your refrigerator so friends can take a peek at it. Pray about how it felt, physically and emotionally, to create a bit of humor. Spend a little time with any heavy feelings you might have experienced when faced with this exercise; where did those feelings originate? Discuss with God the role humor plays in your daily life. Thank God for the gift of laughter and the fresh breezes of creativity.

Today spend thirty minutes on centering prayer.

DAY FIVE

> You are amazing grace. You are unique, unrepeatable, a fragile miracle. You are God's grand and glorious gift. Gifts evoke gifts. And so we who are the gifts of creation now give gifts to our Creator. Let us give with the wild abandon that benefits such examples of amazing grace. Amen.
>
> Sharon Neufer Emswiler and Thomas Neufer Emswiler, "Offertory Prayer"

Contemplation

Do you remember *The Little Drummer Boy*, the animated special shown on television during the Christmas season? Perhaps you can recall that all the boy had to offer the Christ child was the gift of his music. It was not a sweet-voiced violin or a haunting flute melody, but just the rhythm of his simple drum. And that expression of compassion, of joy was enough.

As you sit today, allow a soft hum to echo around in your head, and gently give it voice. Imagine that you are humming with the divine or to the divine, or that perhaps you are allowing the divine to hum through you. Can you feel changes in your body as you explore your own inner melody? What emotions surface for you?

Verbal Prayer

Speak a bit about the experience of finding music within yourself. Pray out any fears you have about humming or singing. Consider the differences you see between passively listening and creating your own music, or between music created to entertain and music created as a way to frame spiritual practice. Write about the ways you could share music in community: through the choir, through singing songs with your kids or grandchildren, or by participating in a nursing home caroling group.

Today spend thirty minutes on centering prayer.

DAY SIX

> The spacious heavens declare the glorious handiwork of God.
> Day and night speak out, although no words are heard.
> They sound their proclamation without the use of speech.
> Their divine direction reaches to the ends of the earth;
> Their message fills the whole world.
>
> Marchiene Vroon Rienstra, "Psalm 19"

Contemplation

If you are able, take a walk outside today. If not, then go to a window, and spend some time looking outside. Take the time to really study what is beyond the windowpane. Do you see something you haven't seen before? If you are able to go out, walk at a speed that allows you to notice the details of your environment; in other words, ask yourself to be present to your environment. Perhaps you will see an odd branch on a familiar tree, a cloud rushing at the fingers of tall office buildings, a gray squirrel holding his meal in his tiny paws, the stems of stubborn grass poking through the sidewalk. Be aware of the season, of how the Spirit is moving through all the earth as you walk. What is it teaching you today? How does your body feel as you concentrate on the sensory impressions arising from your environment? Is your mind more at rest—more peaceful? Are you feeling more grateful, or maybe frustrated by the garbage or less-than-rosy smells you encountered? Take some time to note your impressions in your journal.

Verbal Prayer

Consider the difference between taking a walk to get somewhere and taking a walk with awareness. Muse about how difficult or easy it was to stay focused on your environment: What things helped you stay present?

When did you find your mind wandering? What do these elements tell you about how your mind works? Write down ways you can build little moments of attention into your day. Perhaps you can set your watch to beep each hour, and practice being really aware of your surroundings for a minute. Maybe you can set up a time each day to take a meditative walk, consecrating the time to God.

Today spend thirty minutes on centering prayer.

Week Eight

DAY ONE

> When you aren't distracted by your own negative thinking, when you don't allow yourself to get lost in moments that are gone or yet to come, you are left with this moment.
>
> Sydney Banks, "Cleaning out the Clutter"

Contemplation

As you sit down for your period of prayer today, I invite you to place your hands on your chair or on the floor. Let the experience ground you. Register how the fabric feels against your fingers, how you feel inside when you come into deep contact with reality. What happens to your mind and emotions when you wake up to something as simple as this? Take some time with your journal, and think of at least ten ways that you could wake up during your day. Perhaps you can become deeply aware of setting the table, of walking out to the mailbox, or of pushing the numbers in your building's elevator. How will you be affected by deciding to focus and bringing yourself to the present at points throughout your day?

Verbal Prayer

See if you can recall passages in the sacred literature of the world that speak to the act of being present in our daily life. Consider what might happen if you were more awake and aware with the people you talk to during the day. Might it make a difficult encounter with someone less painful? Pray about any difficulties you had practicing awareness. Write about special moments in your life when you suddenly were deeply present to the moment (like your child's birth, the first sunset you really remember, or holding a loved one's hand as he or she died).

Today spend thirty minutes on centering prayer.

DAY TWO

> Each morning we must hold out the chalice of our being to receive, to carry, to give back.
>
> Dag Hammarskjöld, *Markings*

Contemplation

Today, try to eat an entire meal in silence. This may be difficult if you have small children or if you are used to dinnertime conversation. Perhaps your partner can be convinced to share a lunch in the silence. Or maybe when the kids are off to bed in the evening, you can have a small piece of fruit by yourself, observing silence as you direct all of your attention to your bites. Slow down. Really take time to feel the mechanics of tasting the food, chewing, and swallowing. By giving yourself this precious gift of silence and slowness, you not only better nourish your body but you nourish your soul. Write about the experience in your journal. Does being quiet make you tense? Why? Were you more aware of your food—of the textures and tastes and smells? Were you more aware of the people you dined with? In what ways, if any, did a silent meal feel holy?

Verbal Prayer

Pray about the feelings that arose when you were silent for an entire meal: Was the silence natural or difficult to enter into and maintain? Write a little bit about the moments in your day when you become aware of silence, and what those moments mean to you. Share what you think about the day's quote at the top of the page with someone special to you. Do you agree that a person's spiritual beliefs may influence the course of a disease? Why or why not? How does a meal in silence teach hope?

Today spend thirty minutes on centering prayer.

DAY THREE

> And there he found a certain man named Aeneas, which had kept his bed eight years, and was sick of the palsy. And Peter said unto him, Aeneas, Jesus Christ maketh thee whole: arise and make thy bed. And he arose immediately.
>
> Acts 9:33–34

Contemplation

It is interesting to me that on many occasions when Jesus healed, or others healed in his name, he made his patients "whole." I really prefer the word *whole* to *healed*, because it has a certain roundness to it—a feeling that healing goes beyond the body, to the mind and spirit as well. To arise from a bed, as in the quote above, means to become engaged with the world again in the most elegant and simple ways. It means being able to take meals with loved ones, to move through the world with intention once more. But I also believe a person can be made whole even when the bed remains a reality and sickness a part of life. In this sense, wholeness concerns not just the state of the body but the countenance of the soul as well. And I believe the author of Acts knew this very well.

Today, gather together your drawing materials, and enter into a few minutes of quiet waiting. Ask for an image that captures your own wholeness to be revealed to you. Like exercises we have done before, this image may contain only impressions of color or texture. It may express itself in an abstract symbol or a very concrete image. Represent it as you are able. Again, this picture is for you and your own use. Don't worry about how it looks; it only serves as a touchstone or a reminder for the image you carry within yourself. When you have time, write about the image of "wholeness" in your journal.

Verbal Prayer

Pray about the times you have felt whole, disclosing how this wholeness felt, both emotionally and physically. Consider how you view the differences between being "cured" and being "made whole." Probe any difficulties that arose for you while you worked on this exercise. Act on a way that you could bring the gift of wholeness to someone who is ill. (Activities with sick people might include praying with them, if this is something they are comfortable with; sharing a book; listening to their stories; or simply being present with them without having to fill up the room with talk.)

Today spend thirty minutes on centering prayer.

DAY FOUR

> Wisdom is the olive branch that springeth from the heart,
> bloometh on the tongue, and beareth fruit in the actions.
>
> Elizabeth Grymestom, *Miscellanea, Meditations and Memoratives*

Contemplation

Look carefully at the quote for today. Do you notice that wisdom is equated with an olive branch, the traditional peace offering? That may be the greatest gift of wisdom, the peace that flows from the woman or man who roots the ground of speech and actions in the heart. Today, please consider what words of wisdom your own heart would utter. Take the time to write them in your journal. These words come from the centered, mindful, and wise part of yourself. If no "quotable" words come, try sketching a picture, or describing the feeling state that the word *wisdom* creates in you. Rest secure knowing that we all share the wisdom of our hearts in our own unique ways.

Verbal Prayer

Write a poem or draw a picture that captures your own creative, experiential voice. Pray about the partnership you feel between your voice and the earthy, day-to-day face of Spirit. Hold any uncomfortable feelings and thoughts that might have arisen during this exercise, and then try to voice what was happening to you. Converse with God about any emotional or intellectual differences you feel between your own words of wisdom and the words of someone else.

Today spend thirty minutes on centering prayer.

DAY FIVE

> After silence, that which comes nearest to expressing the inexpressible is music.
>
> Aldous Huxley, *Music at Night*

Contemplation

Today, I ask you simply to sing. Don't worry! You can do it in the shower, or while you are out for a walk, or in the privacy of your living room. You may already sing in a choir or sing professionally. If so, you know a little bit about the joy of using the voice to express the moods of your heart. I challenge you to make up a sacred song to sing, putting your own words to a familiar melody, or maybe just making things up as you go along. Children are usually pretty good at this exercise! At first, you may feel a little foolish, but that will probably pass. Singing opens your throat and expands your lungs, drawing in breath, spirit, life. It gives you an avenue of expression and allows your voice to be heard in a different and beautiful way. Write about your experience of singing your own song in your journal. How did you feel before you sang? Afterward, did you feel any different? Were there physical or emotional changes within you? Did you feel a closer connection with God when you raised your voice in song?

Verbal Prayer

Speak about how it feels to consecrate your own song to the divine. Pray about any difficult feelings that arose when you tried this exercise. Consider ways people can share their own music. Discuss with God how the creative use of voice differs from drawing or writing for you.

Today spend thirty minutes on centering prayer.

DAY SIX

> While we look not at the things which are seen, but at the things which are not seen: for the things which are seen are temporal; but the things which are not seen are eternal.
>
> 2 Corinthians 4:18

Contemplation

I am going to ask you to return to an exercise we did at the very beginning of our journey together. Find a mirror, and take a moment to gaze at your own face. Then, write what you see there now. Are you more aware of the details of your face? Are you able to muster loving kindness or compassion for yourself? Write about this mirror experience in your journal, and then flip back and read what you wrote the first time you did this little exercise (see Week One, Day Six). Has anything changed? Why or why not? Are you able to begin to see in this face a being worthy of love, a being in partnership with the divine? Are you able to take responsibility for this person, who can pass on the gift of love to both self and others?

Verbal Prayer

Pray a prayer of thankfulness for the energy to make this eight-week journey. Share aloud any special insights that have arisen during this time. List the elements of the course that were most important to you, and the ways you plan to continue your explorations in contemplation and holistic health.

Today spend thirty minutes on centering prayer.

Resources

Centering Prayer and the Christian Contemplative Tradition

Goldsmith, Joel S. *The Art of Meditation*. New York: Harper & Row, 1956.

Keating, Thomas. *Open Mind, Open Heart*. New York: Continuum, 2002.

Keating, Thomas, et al. *Finding Grace at the Center*. Still River, MA: St. Bedes Publications, 1978.

Kelsey, Morton T. *The Other Side of Silence*. Mahwah, NJ: Paulist Press, 1976.

Lachman, Barbara. *The Journal of Hildegard of Bingen*. New York: Bell Tower, 1993.

Merton, Thomas. *Life and Holiness*. New York: Image Books, 1996.

———. *Seeds of Contemplation*. Norfolk, CT: New Direction Books, 1949.

———. *Spiritual Direction and Meditation*. Collegeville, MN: Liturgical Press, 1960.

———. *Thoughts in Solitude*. New York: Farrar, Straus and Cudahy, 1956.

"The Method of Centering Prayer." Contemplative Outreach, Ltd., 9 William St., PO Box 737, Butler, NJ 07405. (201) 838-3384. Pamphlet.

Moore, Thomas. *Meditations: On the Monk Who Dwells in Daily Life*. New York: HarperCollins, 1994.

Napier, Nancy J. *Sacred Practices for Conscious Living*. New York: Norton, 1997.

Pennington, M. Basil. *Centered Living: The Way of Centering Prayer*. Liguori, MO: Liguori/Triumph, 1999.

Radice, Betty, ed. *The Cloud of Unknowing and Other Works*. New York: Penguin, 1978.

Rienstra, Marchiene Vroon. *The Swallow's Nest: A Feminine Reading of the Psalms*. Grand Rapids, MI: Eerdmans, 1992.

Roberts, Bernadette. *The Path to No-Self: Life at the Center*. Albany: State University of New York Press, 1991.

Sinetar, Marsha. *Ordinary People as Monks and Mystics*. New York: Paulist Press, 1986.

Trembley, Lo-Ann, and David Trembley. *Pray with All Your Senses: Discovering the Wholeness Jesus Brings*. Chicago: ACTA Press, 1997.

Vennard, Jane E. *Praying with Body and Soul*. Minneapolis: Augsburg Press, 1998.

Wuellner, Flora Slosson. *Prayer and Our Bodies*. Nashville, TN: Upper Room, 1987.

Elements of Holistic Health Care

Balch, Phyllis A., and James Balch. *Prescription for Dietary Wellness*. New York: Books for Health, 1987.

Boston Women's Health Collective. *Our Bodies, Ourselves for the New Century*. New York: Touchstone Books, 1998.

Capellini, Steve, and Michel VanWelden. *Massage for Dummies*. New York: IDG Books, 1999.

Duyff, Roberta Larson. *The American Dietetic Association's Complete Food and Nutrition Guide*. Minneapolis: Chronimed Publishing, 1998.

Edlin, Gordon, Eric Golanty, and Kelli Brown. *Health and Wellness*. Sudbury, MA: Jones and Bartlett, 1996.

Gottlieb, Bill. *New Choices in Natural Healing*. New York: Rodale Press, 1995.

Levine, Andrew, and Valerie Lavine. *The Bodywork and Massage Sourcebook*. Los Angeles: Lowell House, 1999.

Lidell, Lucinda. *The Book of Massage*. New York: Simon & Schuster, 1984.

Lipson, Elaine Marie. *The Organic Foods Sourcebook*. New York: Contemporary Books, 2001.

Mumford, Susan. *The Complete Book of Massage*. New York: Plume Books, 1995.

Pitchford, Paul. *Healing with Whole Foods*. Berkeley, CA: North Atlantic Books, 1993.

Rossman, Martin L. *Guided Imagery for Self-Healing*. Tiburon, CA: H. J. Kramer Books, 2000.

St. James, Elaine. *Inner Simplicity*. New York: Hyperion, 1995.

Staphaniak, Joanne. *Being Vegan*. Los Angeles: Lowell House, 2000.

Humor

Cousins, Norman. *Head First: The Biology of Hope and the Healing Power of the Human Spirit*. New York: Penguin Press, 1990.

Dove, Pragito. *Lunchtime Enlightenment*. New York: Viking, Compass, 2001.

The Humor Project. 110 Spring St., Saratoga Springs, NY 12866. Publishes titles concerning theory, research, and practical benefits of humor.

Mindfulness, Meditation, and Health

Ardinger, Barbara. *Goddess Meditations*. St. Paul, MN: Llewellyn Publications, 1998.

Benson, Herbert. *Timeless Healing*. New York: Simon and Schuster, 1996.

Borysenko, Joan. *Minding the Body, Mending the Mind*. New York: Bantam, 1988.

Carlson, Richard, and Benjamin Shield, eds. *Handbook for the Soul*. Boston: Little, Brown, 1995.

Coles, Robert. *The Spiritual Life of Children*. New York: Houghton Mifflin, 1990.

Davich, Victor N. *The Best Guide to Meditation*. Los Angeles: Renaissance Books, 1998.

Gunaratana, Henepola. *Mindfulness in Plain English*. Somerville, MA: Wisdom Publications, 1991.

Gandhi, M. K. *Vows and Observances*. Berkeley, CA: Berkeley Hills Books, 1999.

Hahn, Thich Nhat. *Living Buddha, Living Christ*. New York: Riverhead Books, 1995.

———. *Present Moment, Wonderful Moment*. Berkeley, CA: Parallax Press, 1990.

———. *Sun in My Heart*. Berkeley, CA: Parallax Press, 1988.

Harvey, John. *The Quiet Mind*. Honesdale, PA: Himalayan Institute, 1988.

Judith, Anodea. *Wheels of Life*. St. Paul, MN: Llewellyn Publications, 1999.

Kabat-Zinn, Jon. *Full Catastrophe Living*. New York: Dell, Delta Books, 1990.

———. *Wherever You Go, There You Are*. New York: Hyperion, 1994.

Kennedy, Robert E. *Zen Spirit, Christian Spirit*. New York: Continuum, 1996.

Muller, Wayne. *Legacy of the Heart*. New York: Simon and Schuster, 1992.

Seaward, Brian Luke. *Stand Like Mountain, Flow Like Water*. Deerfield, FL: Health Communications, 1996.

Welwood, John. *Ordinary Magic*. Boston: Shambhala Publications, 1992.

Music Therapy

For a complete listing of available resources, contact the American Association for Music Therapy, PO Box 80012, Valley Forge, PA 19484. (215) 265-4006.

Campbell, Don G. *The Mozart Effect for Children*. New York: Avon Books, 1997.

———. *The Mozart Effect: Music for Children*. New York: Quill, 1997.

Dewhurst-Maddock, Olivia. *The Book of Sound Therapy: Heal Yourself with Music and Voice*. New York: Fireside Books, 1993.

Gardner, Kay. *Sounding the Inner Landscape: Music as Medicine*. Rockport, MA: Element Books, 1997.

Williamson, Marianne. *Healing: Music, Meditation and Prayer*. Carlsbad, CA: Hay House Audio, 1997.

Vegetarian Recipes and Guidebooks

Greenberg, Patricia. *The Whole Soy Cookbook*. New York: Three Rivers Press, 1998.

Leavy, Herbert T. *Vegetarian Times Cookbook*. New York: Collier Books, 1984.

Moon, Rosemary. *Classic Vegetarian Cuisine*. New York: Smithmark Publishing, 1995.

Moosewood Collective. *Moosewood Restaurant Low-Fat Favorites*. New York: Clarkson Potter Publishing, 1996.

Robbins, John. *May All Be Fed: Diet for a New World*. New York: Avon, 1992.

Spitler, Sue. *1,001 Low-Fat Vegetarian Recipes*. Chicago: Surrey Books, 2000.

Tracy, Lisa. *The Gradual Vegetarian: The Step by Step Way to Start Eating the Right Stuff Today*. New York: Dell, 1985.

Writing and Journaling

Dorff, Francis. *Simply Soul Stirring: Writing as a Meditative Practice*. New York: Paulist Press, 1998.

Goldberg, Natalie. *Thunder and Lightning*. New York: Bantam, 2000.

———. *Wild Mind*. Boston: Shambhala Publications, 1991.

———. *Writing Down the Bones*. Boston: Shambhala Publications, 1986.

Klug, Ronald. *How to Keep a Spiritual Journal*. Minneapolis: Augsburg Books, 1993.

Progoff, Ira. *At a Journal Workshop*. New York: Dialogue House, 1975.

Yoga and Stretching

Anderson, Bob, and Jean E. Anderson. *Stretch*. Bolinas, CA: Shelter Publications, 1987.

Anderson, Sandra, and Rolf Sovik. *Yoga: Mastering the Basics*. Honesdale, PA: Himalayan Press, 2000.

Aurobindo, Shri. *Synthesis of Yoga*. Pondicherry, India: Shri Aurobindo Ashram, 1971.

Devi, Nischala Joy. *The Healing Path of Yoga*. New York: Three Rivers Press, 2000.

Farhi, Donna. *Yoga Mind, Body and Spirit: A Return to Wholeness*. New York: Owl Books, 2000.

Kraftsow, Gary. *Yoga for Transformation*. New York: Penguin Compass, 2002.

Lasater, Judith. *Relax and Renew: Restful Yoga for Stressful Times*. New York: Rodmell Press, 1995.

Ryan, Thomas. *Prayer of Heart and Body: Mediation and Yoga as Christian Spiritual Practice*. Mahwah, NJ: Paulist Press, 1991.

Schaeffer, Rachel. *Yoga for Your Spiritual Muscles*. Wheaton, IL: Quest Books, 1998.

Schiffman, Erich. *Yoga: The Spirit and Practice of Moving into Stillness*. New York: Pocket Books, 1996.

Weller, Stella. *Yoga Therapy*. New York: HarperCollins, 1995.